THE NEW YORK YANKEES

Sloan MacRae

PowerKiDS press.

New York

Published in 2010 by The Rosen Publishing Group, Inc.
29 East 21st Street, New York, NY 10010

First Edition

Editor: Amelie von Zumbusch
Book Design: Greg Tucker
Photo Researcher: Jessica Gerweck

Photo Credits: Cover Shutterstock.com; cover (Derek Jeter), pp. 5, 21, 22 (bottom) Al Bello/Getty Images; cover (Mickey Mantle, Babe Ruth, Yogi Berra), pp. 13, 15, 22 (top) Hulton Archive/Getty Images; p. 7 © Michael Yamashita/Corbis; pp. 9, 19 Jim McIsaac/Getty Images; p. 11 Mark Rucker/Transcendental Graphics/Getty Images; p. 17 © Neal Preston/Corbis.

Library of Congress Cataloging-in-Publication Data

MacRae, Sloan.
   The New York Yankees / Sloan MacRae. — 1st ed.
      p. cm. — (America's greatest teams)
   Includes index.
   ISBN 978-1-4042-8129-5 (library binding) — ISBN 978-1-4358-3390-6 (pbk.) —
ISBN 978-1-4358-3391-3 (6-pack)
   1. New York Yankees (Baseball team)—History—Juvenile literature. I. Title.
   GV875.N4M32 2010
   796.357'64097471—dc22
                                        2009004851

Manufactured in the United States of America

CONTENTS

A GREAT BASEBALL TEAM

What makes a baseball team great? It might be great **athletes**. It could also be the number of World Series **championships** the team has won. These are just two of the things that make the New York Yankees a great baseball team. Some of the greatest baseball players of all time have been Yankees. In fact, the very first baseball superstar, Babe Ruth, was a Yankee.

The World Series is Major League Baseball's championship. The Yankees have won more World Series titles than any other baseball team. Many sports writers and fans believe that the Yankees are the greatest American sports team of all time.

The Yankees have talented players from countries around the world on their team. For example, designated hitter Hideki Matsui (far left) comes from Japan.

THE BRONX BOMBERS

The Yankees have two well-known **logos**. One is a red, white, and blue hat sitting on a baseball bat. The other is the letter *Y* overlapping the letter *N*. The letters stand for "New York." This logo appears on the team's home uniforms, which are white with navy blue **pinstripes**. When a player joins the team, people say he is now "wearing pinstripes." The Yankees' owner likes the players to be clean-cut. This means they cannot have long hair or beards.

The Yankees' ballpark is in a New York City neighborhood called the Bronx. The Yankees are nicknamed the Bronx Bombers because the team has so many power hitters.

The old Yankee Stadium, seen here, was the Yankees' home from 1923 to 2008. In 2009, the new Yankee Stadium opened nearby.

NEW YORK FANS

The Bronx Bombers have some of the most **passionate** fans in baseball. The Yankees' biggest **rivals** are the Boston Red Sox. Yankees fans and Red Sox fans often tease and argue with each other. The loudest Yankees fans are known as the Bleacher Creatures. They **chant** the name of every Yankee player at the beginning of the game. The Bleacher Creatures sit near the right-field wall. They often make fun of the **opposing** team's right fielder.

The Yankees also have some very famous fans. Movie star Billy Crystal, rock star Bob Dylan, and former New York City mayor Rudy Giuliani all root for the Yankees.

The Yankees have many fans, both young and old. Each season since 1999, this popular team has drawn a total of more than three million fans to Yankee Stadium.

9

THE NEW YORK HIGHLANDERS

The Yankees did not begin their history in New York. At first, the team played in Baltimore and was called the Orioles. Today, Baltimore has another team called the Orioles. However, fans of these new Orioles boo the Yankees.

In 1903, the old Orioles moved to a ballpark called Hilltop Park in New York City. After this move, the team was called the New York Highlanders since they played high on a hill. The Highlanders changed their name to the Yankees in 1913. That year, the team moved to a stadium called the Polo Grounds. The Polo Grounds was not on a hill. Therefore, the name Highlanders no longer made sense.

Here are some of the members of the New York Highlanders during the team's first season in New York.

THE BABE AND THE IRON HORSE

In 1920, the Boston Red Sox made a deal to trade Babe Ruth to the Yankees. Ruth became a superstar, setting a record in the 1927 season with 60 **home runs**. The Yankees became so **popular** that they needed a new stadium to hold all their fans. In 1923, Yankee Stadium was built in the Bronx. It was known as the house that Ruth built because it was built with money that Ruth's popularity brought to the team.

One of Ruth's most talented teammates was Lou Gehrig. Gehrig was called the Iron Horse for playing 2,130 games in a row without taking a day off. He still holds the record for the most **grand slams**.

Ruth (right) and Gehrig (left) played over 70 years ago. However, they are still considered to be two of baseball's all-time top players.

BASEBALL'S GREATEST TEAM

Ruth and Gehrig **retired** in the 1930s, but Joe DiMaggio became the Yankees' next superstar slugger, or hitter. DiMaggio made history in the 1941 season by getting a hit in 56 **consecutive** games. This is still a major-league record.

Over the next 10 years, Mickey Mantle, Yogi Berra, and Whitey Ford joined the team and became new stars. The Yankees won five World Series in a row from 1949 to 1953. They were baseball's greatest team. In 1956, pitcher Don Larsen threw the only perfect game in World Series history. A perfect game happens when none of the opposing players safely reach first base.

Catcher Yogi Berra is known both for being a wild swinger and for the funny things he said. These funny sayings became know as Yogi-isms.

THE M&M BOYS AND MR. OCTOBER

During the 1961 season, Yankees sluggers Mickey Mantle and Roger Maris made baseball history. Due to their names, Maris and Mantle were called the M&M Boys. In 1961, the M&M Boys hit home runs at such a fast rate that fans thought one of them would break Babe Ruth's record of 60 home runs. In the very last game of the season, Maris hit his sixty-first home run and broke Ruth's record.

In 1973, a businessman named George Steinbrenner bought the Yankees. A few years later, outfielder Reggie Jackson joined the team. Jackson earned the nickname Mr. October for playing so well in World Series games, which take place in October.

Reggie Jackson's great batting skills earned him the title of most valuable player in the 1977 World Series. The Yankees beat the Los Angeles Dodgers to win the series.

ANOTHER YANKEE NAMED JOE

The Yankees had a great first baseman named Don Mattingly during the 1980s and early 1990s. Sadly, Mattingly and the Yankees did not win any World Series titles. In 1996, the team's luck changed when Joe Torre became the Yankees' **manager**.

New York newspapers made fun of Steinbrenner for hiring Torre. They called Torre Clueless Joe because he had not had much success before joining the Yankees. Torre soon proved himself. The Yankees reached the **postseason** every year that he was their manager. They won four World Series in the late 1990s and early 2000s. Torre found several new stars, such as Derek Jeter, who became a Yankee in 1995.

Joe Torre managed the Yankees for 12 years. Here, Torre (right) argues with an umpire. Umpires are the people who rule on plays in a game.

A NEW HOME

The 2008 season was **bittersweet** for the Yankees. Torre left the team, and they failed to make the postseason for the first time in 13 years. They also said good-bye to their home. The Yankees played their final game in the old Yankee Stadium on September 21, 2008. It was against the Baltimore Orioles. In 2009, the Bombers moved into a new stadium across the street.

The Yankees are North America's most successful sports team. They have more championship titles than any American baseball, football, basketball, or hockey team. Today's star players, such as Derek Jeter and Alex Rodriguez, will help them win more.

The 2008 Yankees posed for reporters after winning their very last game in Yankee Stadium. The Yankees beat the Orioles, 7–3.

NEW YORK YANKEES TIMELINE

1913
The Highlanders change their name to the Yankees.

1903
The Baltimore Orioles move to New York City and become the New York Highlanders.

1920
The Red Sox make a deal to send Babe Ruth to the Yankees.

1961
Roger Maris hits his sixty-first home run of the season and breaks Babe Ruth's record.

1956
Don Larsen pitches the only perfect game in World Series history.

1962
The Yankees play their longest game in team history, against the Detroit Tigers. The game lasts 22 innings.

1977
Reggie Jackson hits three home runs in Game Six of the World Series.

2000
The Yankees beat the New York Mets in the World Series. It is a Subway Series, or a series in which both teams are from New York City.

2004
Pitchers Mike Mussina and Kevin Brown win their two-hundredth victories in back-to-back games.

2008
The Yankees beat the Orioles in the final game at Yankee Stadium.

GLOSSARY

ATHLETES (ATH-leets) People who take part in sports.

BITTERSWEET (BIH-ter-sweet) Both happy and sad.

CHAMPIONSHIPS (CHAM-pee-un-ships) Contests held to decide the best, or the winner.

CHANT (CHANT) To say words over and over without changing tone.

CONSECUTIVE (ken-SEH-kyuh-tiv) In a row, or back to back.

GRAND SLAMS (GRAND SLAMZ) Home runs hit when someone is on every base.

HOME RUNS (HOME RUNZ) Hits in which the batter touches all the bases and scores one or more runs.

LOGOS (LOH-gohz) Pictures or words that stand for a team or company.

MANAGER (MA-nih-jer) The person in charge of training a team.

OPPOSING (uh-POH-zing) On the opposite side in a game.

PASSIONATE (PA-shun-et) Full of strong feeling.

PINSTRIPES (PIN-stryps) Thin lines, often on clothing.

POPULAR (PAH-pyuh-lur) Liked by lots of people.

POSTSEASON (pohst-SEE-zun) Games played after the regular season.

RETIRED (rih-TY-urd) Gave up an office or job.

RIVALS (RY-vulz) People or teams who try to get or do the same thing as one another.

INDEX

WEB SITES

Due to the changing nature of Internet links, PowerKids Press has developed an online list of Web sites related to the subject of this book. This site is updated regularly. Please use this link to access the list:
www.powerkidslinks.com/teams/nyy/